Spring

Signs of the Season
Around North America

Written by Valerie J. Gerard   Illustrated by Eric Thomas

Content Advisor: Julie Dunlap, Ph.D. • Reading Advisor: Lauren A. Liang, M.A.
Literacy Education, University of Minnesota, Minneapolis, Minnesota

PICTURE WINDOW BOOKS
MINNEAPOLIS, MINNESOTA

To Hoddy and Charlotte, my best friends—V.J.G.

Editor: Nadia Higgins
Designer: Melissa Voda
Page production: The Design Lab
The illustrations in this book were prepared digitally.

Picture Window Books
5115 Excelsior Boulevard
Suite 232
Minneapolis, MN 55416
1-877-845-8392
www.picturewindowbooks.com

Printed in the United States of America.

Library of Congress Cataloging-in-Publication Data
Gerard, Valerie J., 1959–
  Spring: signs of the season around North America / written by Valerie J. Gerard ; illustrated by Eric Thomas.
    p. cm. — (Through the seasons) Includes index.
  Summary: Examines how spring brings observable changes in weather, nature, and people.
  ISBN 1-4048-0002-6 (library binding : alk. paper)
  1. Spring—North America—Juvenile literature. [1. Spring.] I. Thomas, Eric, ill. II. Title. III. Through the seasons (Minneapolis, Minn.)
  QB637.5 .G47 2003
  508.2—dc2   2002005842

One way to mark the seasons is by looking at the calendar. The calendar dates are based on Earth's yearly trip around the sun. In North America, spring begins on March 19, 20, or 21, when day and night are about the same length. Throughout spring, the days keep getting longer.

Another way to mark the seasons is to look around you at the changes in weather and nature. In North America, the first signs of spring appear in the south, then move north. This book helps you to see the signs of spring in different places around North America.

Slushy sidewalks, mushy mud, melting snow, and sprinkling rain. Flowers are blooming, birds are calling. Each day is a little longer and a little warmer. Spring is here.

Spring isn't the same everywhere in North America. What happens in spring where you live?

Look in the back for a spring activity.

Spring comes early to the desert, with strong winds.

Lizards and snakes stretch out on sun-warmed rocks.

Scorpions and beetles scurry in the sand.

New life is everywhere.

FUN FACT:
The desert is mostly brown and dull green in spring until the cactuses bloom. Many cactus flowers last only a few days.

In the Appalachian Mountains, gentle rain and warm sunshine make flowers, trees, and bushes bloom.

The noisy birds poke in the grass. They are looking for food to feed their babies.

In California, spring breezes blow in cool air from the ocean. The driftwood and seashells along the shore were left by winter storms.

In spring, gray whales lead their babies north from California to their summer homes in Alaska. The whales leap out of the water and fall back in with a splash.

Lightning bolts flash in the midwestern sky.

Rumbling thunder rattles the dishes.

Rivers rush and roar. The water is high from all the rain and melting snow. Sometimes rivers flood.

FUN FACT:
Hailstones are small balls of ice that fall from the sky during some thunderstorms. They can be as big as golf balls.

After a storm, the air smells clean. It's time to go outside!
Children fly kites that dip and swoop in the sky.

Birds circle and flutter behind the tractors as farmers plow the fields. The birds land and snatch up worms from the freshly turned soil.

FUN FACT:
In spring, monarch butterflies return from their winter homes in Mexico and California. They land on milkweed plants and lay eggs.

13

See the tiny green shoots poking up through the snow? In New England, crocuses are one of the first signs that spring is here.

14

Soon the snow begins to melt. Better wear your rubber boots!
Mud is everywhere.

Get out your bicycle and go for a ride.

People walk in the parks. They feed the ducks.

Children run, climb, and slide at the playground.

The sidewalks are spotted with shade from new leaves.

Little by little, the brown grass turns green.

FUN FACT:

As the soil warms up, earthworms wiggle to the top from their deep winter resting places. After it rains, they squirm on the sidewalks.

Spring comes last to northern Canada and Alaska. The days are getting very long. The nights are just a few hours long.

FUN FACT:
Thick ice on lakes and rivers cracks and breaks as it melts, making a loud noise.

18

Grizzly bears and other winter sleepers wake up hungry.

Beavers and wolves are busy caring for their young.

Now you know what spring is like In different places around North America. What happens in spring where you live?

FUN FACT:
Spring is a time for celebrating. Many people celebrate religious holidays like Easter and Passover. On Memorial Day, people in the United States remember soldiers who died in wars. Canadians have a holiday on Victoria Day. Mexicans celebrate Cinco de Mayo.

DESERTS

Nogales, Mexico

Average high April temperature: 77°F/25°C

Hours of daylight on April 10th: 12 hours, 48 minutes

What to wear: windbreaker

Sign of spring: gusty winds

APPALACHIAN MOUNTAINS

Asheville, North Carolina

Average high April temperature: 68°F/20°C

Hours of daylight on April 10th: 12 hours, 55 minutes

What to wear: rain gear

Sign of spring: gentle rains

CALIFORNIA COAST

Santa Barbara, California

Average high April temperature: 67°F/19°C

Hours of daylight on April 10th: 12 hours, 53 minutes

What to wear: rain slicker, sweater

Sign of spring: whales

MIDWEST

Des Moines, Iowa

Average high April temperature: 61°F/16°C

Hours of daylight on April 10th: 13 hours, 7 minutes

What to wear: sweatshirt, raincoat

Sign of spring: thunderstorms

NEW ENGLAND

Burlington, Vermont

Average high April temperature: 53°F/12°C

Hours of daylight on April 10th: 13 hours, 13 minutes

What to wear: light sweater or raincoat

Sign of spring: mud

ALASKA/NORTHERN CANADA

Fairbanks, Alaska

Average high April temperature: 41°F/5°C

Hours of daylight on April 10th: 14 hours, 38 minutes

What to wear: light jacket, sweater

Sign of spring: breaking ice

Be a Nature Detective!

Look under a log. Roll away a rock. You will see insects scrambling to hide themselves. What kinds of bugs did you see? Poke the log and the dirt with a stick. Do you see any insect eggs?

Look closely at the ground. After it rains, you might see little piles of dirt around a hole. There could be an earthworm there. Can you find bugs in the grass? You might see ants, spiders, and beetles.

Listen for birds calling and singing. Look around. Watch for birds gathering twigs and bits of strings for their nests. What other things are they gathering? Where are they building their nests? Look for bird eggshells and feathers on the ground. Bird nests may be nearby. Pay special attention early in the morning or after it rains. That is when birds are busiest.

Words to Know

Cinco de Mayo—a Mexican festival, observed on May 5th

crocuses—white, yellow, or purple flowers that bloom in very early spring

driftwood—pieces of wood that have floated in the water for a long time. The water has smoothed the pieces of wood into odd and interesting shapes.

Easter—a Christian holiday

hailstones—pieces of ice that fall from the sky during thunderstorms

Passover—a Jewish holiday

spring—the season between winter and summer. In North America, it lasts from the end of March to the end of June.

To Learn More

AT THE LIBRARY

Carr, Jan. *Splish, Splash, Spring.* New York: Holiday House, 2001.

Peters, Lisa Westberg. *Cold Little Duck, Duck, Duck.* New York: Greenwillow Books, 2000.

Schnur, Steven. *Spring: An Alphabet Acrostic.* New York: Clarion Books, 1999.

Seuling, Barbara. *Spring Song.* San Diego: Harcourt Brace, 2001.

Stille, Darlene R. *Spring.* Minneapolis: Compass Point Books, 2001.

FACT HOUND

Fact Hound offers a safe, fun way to find Web sites related to this book. All of the sites on Fact Hound have been researched by our staff.

http://www.facthound.com

1. Visit the Fact Hound home page.
2. Enter a search word related to this book, or type in this special code: 1404800026
3. Click the FETCH IT button.

Your trusty Fact Hound will fetch the best sites for you!

Index